20 Day Sex Challenge For Couples!

Copyright © 2020 by Blue Rock Couple Workbooks

All rights reserved. This book or any portion thereof may not be reproduced or used in any manner whatsoever without the express written permission of the publisher except for the use of brief quotations in a book review.

Printed in the United States of America

How to use this book:

Everyone knows that being a couple, married or not, takes work. That's why this workbook is designed to ignite or reignite sex in a marriage or serious relationship.

There is a mixture of sexual items on the list, some are in the bedroom, while some will challenge you outside the bedroom.

This can be done 20 consecutive days, you can do every other day, or whatever works for you.

Each day there is a conversation starter, or activity in or out of the bedroom to do. Simply complete the conversation or activity and then each of you write down your reaction. This forces the conversation and activity being done!

This challenge can then be repeated as often as needed to increase sex and intimacy!

Let's begin!

Day 1

Share with each other your favorite sexual memory together.

Tonight, reenact those memories for some sexual fun!

Her Reaction

_____
_____
_____
_____
_____
_____
_____
_____

His Reaction

_____
_____
_____
_____
_____
_____
_____
_____

Do This Again Sometime?

Yes ☐   No ☐

Day 3

What is the most public place you've had sex before?

In the next 24 hours, have sex again in a similar public place!

Her Reaction

_____
_____
_____
_____
_____
_____
_____
_____

His Reaction

_____
_____
_____
_____
_____
_____
_____
_____

Do This Again Sometime?

Yes ☐   No ☐

Day 4

Tonight at bedtime, wear something very sexy to bed, and have sex while having some of that sexy clothing on.

Her Reaction

_____
_____
_____
_____
_____
_____
_____
_____

His Reaction

_____
_____
_____
_____
_____
_____
_____
_____

Do This Again Sometime?

Yes ☐   No ☐

Day 5

In the next 24 hours, have a quickie OUTSIDE the bedroom.

The couch, kitchen, outside, etc..

Her Reaction

_____
_____
_____
_____
_____
_____
_____
_____

His Reaction

_____
_____
_____
_____
_____
_____
_____
_____

Do This Again Sometime?

Yes ☐   No ☐

Day 6

Share with each other your favorite sex positions.

Tonight, have sex while incorporating both of these positions

Her Reaction

_____
_____
_____
_____
_____
_____
_____
_____

His Reaction

_____
_____
_____
_____
_____
_____
_____
_____

Do This Again Sometime?

Yes ☐   No ☐

Day 7

Light some candles, put on soft music, and have some slow, sensual sex.

Her Reaction

_____
_____
_____
_____
_____
_____
_____
_____

His Reaction

_____
_____
_____
_____
_____
_____
_____
_____

Do This Again Sometime?

Yes ☐   No ☐

Day 8

Morning sex! Wake up and have sex before doing anything else.

Wake your partner up by giving them oral!

Her Reaction

_____
_____
_____
_____
_____
_____
_____
_____

His Reaction

_____
_____
_____
_____
_____
_____
_____
_____

Do This Again Sometime?

Yes ☐   No ☐

Day 9

Give him a handjob only, no sex. Edge him, and tease him to make him last.

Her Reaction

_____
_____
_____
_____
_____
_____
_____
_____

His Reaction

_____
_____
_____
_____
_____
_____
_____
_____

Do This Again Sometime?

Yes ☐   No ☐

Day 10

Incorporate the 69 position to some sex tonight.

Her Reaction

His Reaction

Do This Again Sometime?

Yes ☐   No ☐

Day 11

Have sex while taking photos/videos.

Extra points to dress up for the camera!

Her Reaction

_____
_____
_____
_____
_____
_____
_____
_____

His Reaction

_____
_____
_____
_____
_____
_____
_____
_____

Do This Again Sometime?

Yes ☐   No ☐

Day 12

Watch some porn
together while
masturbating together.
No sex!

Her Reaction

_____
_____
_____
_____
_____
_____
_____

His Reaction

_____
_____
_____
_____
_____
_____
_____

Do This Again Sometime?

Yes ☐   No ☐

Day 13

Incorporate a sex toy into the bedroom for a steamy sex session.

Her Reaction

_____
_____
_____
_____
_____
_____
_____
_____

His Reaction

_____
_____
_____
_____
_____
_____
_____
_____

Do This Again Sometime?

Yes ☐   No ☐

Day 14

Take a shower together and have sex or oral sex.

Her Reaction

_____
_____
_____
_____
_____
_____
_____
_____

His Reaction

_____
_____
_____
_____
_____
_____
_____
_____

Do This Again Sometime?

Yes ☐   No ☐

Day 15

In the next 24 hours, fool around in the car sexually or just make out.

Her Reaction

His Reaction

Do This Again Sometime?

Yes ☐   No ☐

Day 16

Give her sexual pleasure by just fingering her to orgasm. No sex!

Tease and edge her to climax.

Her Reaction

___
___
___
___
___
___
___
___

His Reaction

___
___
___
___
___
___
___
___

Do This Again Sometime?

Yes ☐   No ☐

Day 17

Have sex while roleplaying. Maybe she can be the cleaner or he can be the landscaper.

Her Reaction

_____
_____
_____
_____
_____
_____
_____
_____

His Reaction

_____
_____
_____
_____
_____
_____
_____
_____

Do This Again Sometime?

Yes ☐   No ☐

Day 18

Go to an Adult Shop together and shop for a new toy or accessories.

Bonus for going to a shop with preview booths for fooling around in booths

Her Reaction

_____
_____
_____
_____
_____
_____
_____
_____

His Reaction

_____
_____
_____
_____
_____
_____
_____
_____

Do This Again Sometime?

Yes ☐   No ☐

Day 19

Spend an evening together naked around the house, followed by some great sex.

Her Reaction

_____
_____
_____
_____
_____
_____
_____

His Reaction

_____
_____
_____
_____
_____
_____
_____

Do This Again Sometime?

Yes ☐   No ☐

Day 20

Share with each other your reflections and favorite parts of this challenge.

Her Reaction

_____
_____
_____
_____
_____
_____
_____
_____

His Reaction

_____
_____
_____
_____
_____
_____
_____
_____

Do This Again Sometime?

Yes ☐   No ☐

Made in the USA
Columbia, SC
13 January 2025